Cut peridot gemstone

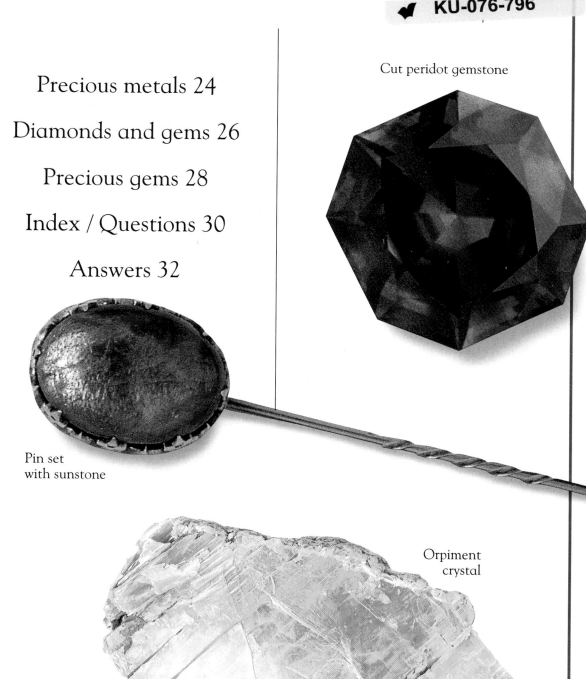

Pin set
with sunstone

Orpiment
crystal

Tut's treasure

In November 1922, the English archaeologist Howard Carter found the tomb of the Egyptian king, or pharaoh, Tutankhamun. It had been hidden for 3,200 years!

Mummy case
Tutankhamun was placed in three coffins, one inside the other. The inner one was made of solid gold and contained the preserved body, or mummy, of the king.

Golden shrine
Four golden shrines stood around the pharaoh's coffin. Behind their swinging doors sat sacred statues.

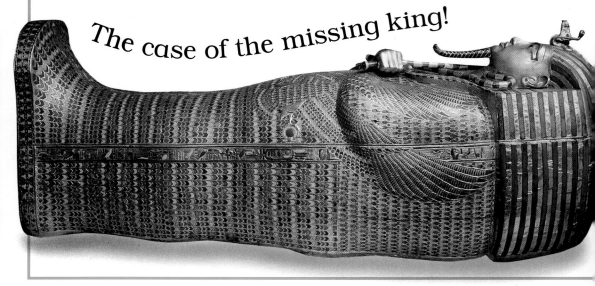

The case of the missing king!

Gold record

The pharaoh's mummy wore a mask of solid gold inlaid with gems. It shows how young Tutankhamun looked when he died. He was probably no older than 20.

All Egyptian kings wore a striped headdress

Where's my mummy?

Not only pharaohs, but most rich Egyptians were mummified after death. Their bodies were meant to last for ever.

Decorated with religious symbols

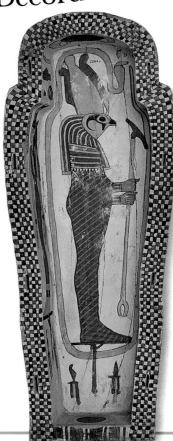

Mummy cases

Message boxes
Mummy cases were painted with scenes from the afterlife.

Last supper
Ancient Egyptians believed that the dead person could still eat and drink in the afterlife.

Hard at work ...after death!

Say "aahh"
After death, these tools were used in a special ceremony called the Opening of the Mouth to help the mummy "eat and drink".

No rest for some
Mummies were often buried with models of workers, called *shabtis*, who carried farming tools. Shabtis served their masters after death.

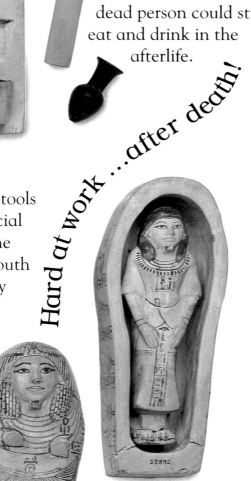

This wooden mummy case was painted gold to make it look much finer

9

The riches of Greece

We can learn a lot about people who lived in the past through the treasures we find, from fabulous ornaments to everyday things. The objects shown here all date from the time of the ancient Greeks.

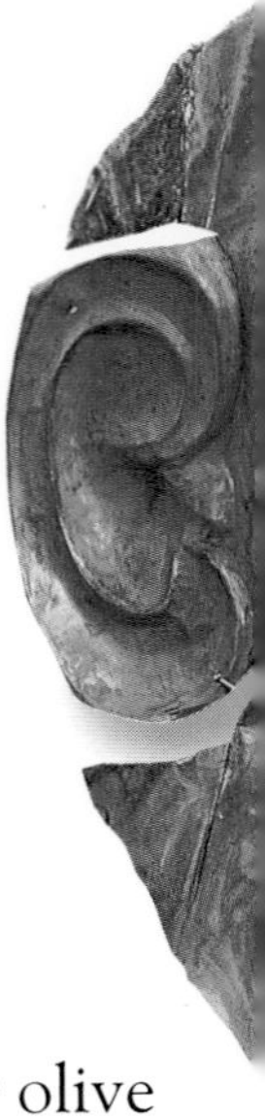

Meals that were swimming in oil

Oil's well in the kitchen
This little dolphin is a container for olive oil. The ancient Greeks were a seafaring people who respected the dolphins that swam around their coasts.

Dolphin oil container

Whose mask?
This gold mask was found in Mycenae, Greece. It was once thought to be Agamemnon, a Greek king. But the true answer remains a mystery.

This owl is a symbol of the goddess Athena

The face of a 3,600 year-old king?

This coin is from the isle of Aegina

Spare change
The Greeks were the first people to use coins. They made them out of gold or silver, and stamped them with symbols of their gods.

Roman treasure

Treasures that belonged to Roman citizens 2,000 years ago tell us many things, from what people wore to the amount of money that they earned.

Golden wonders
Beautifully crafted earrings like these were worn by the rich women of ancient Rome.

The Roman empire stretched ...

Back pay
This hoard of gold coins was over four years' pay for a Roman soldier. It was buried in England and then forgotten.

These solid gold earrings are shaped like dolphins

Arm bag

Roman soldiers carried their money in a small leather or metal purse worn on the arm like a bracelet. The lid faced in, so the purse could only be opened when it was taken off.

The head of the emperor and his honorary titles

Lid

across Europe, Africa and the Middle East

Roman sword scabbard

Present swords!

This unusual scabbard was presented to a soldier by a grateful Emperor Tiberius. It is made of wood and richly decorated with gold and silver.

A portrait of Emperor Tiberius

13

American gold

In the years before Columbus reached America in 1492, three great civilizations flourished in the areas of Mexico, Central America, and Peru: the Aztec, the Maya, and the Inca.

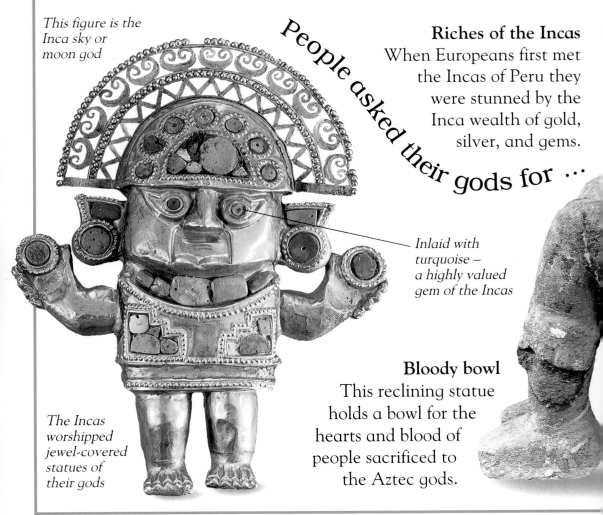

This figure is the Inca sky or moon god

People asked their gods for …

Riches of the Incas
When Europeans first met the Incas of Peru they were stunned by the Inca wealth of gold, silver, and gems.

Inlaid with turquoise – a highly valued gem of the Incas

The Incas worshipped jewel-covered statues of their gods

Bloody bowl
This reclining statue holds a bowl for the hearts and blood of people sacrificed to the Aztec gods.

Dog bites man

This fierce coyote mask from the Central American city of Tula was worn by a warrior. It is decorated with mother-of-pearl.

Statue guarded the shrine of "Tlaloc", the god of rain

good crops and a healthy life

Chacmool – a sacrificial statue

Funny money

Money doesn't have to be made out of gold or silver to be valuable. After all, today we use paper or plastic to buy things. But teeth, shells, and stones have also been used as money!

For some peoples, perforated stones, teeth, and ...

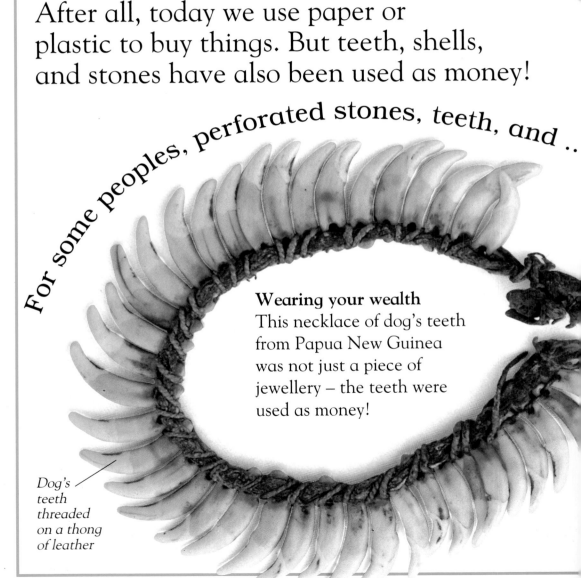

Wearing your wealth
This necklace of dog's teeth from Papua New Guinea was not just a piece of jewellery – the teeth were used as money!

Dog's teeth threaded on a thong of leather

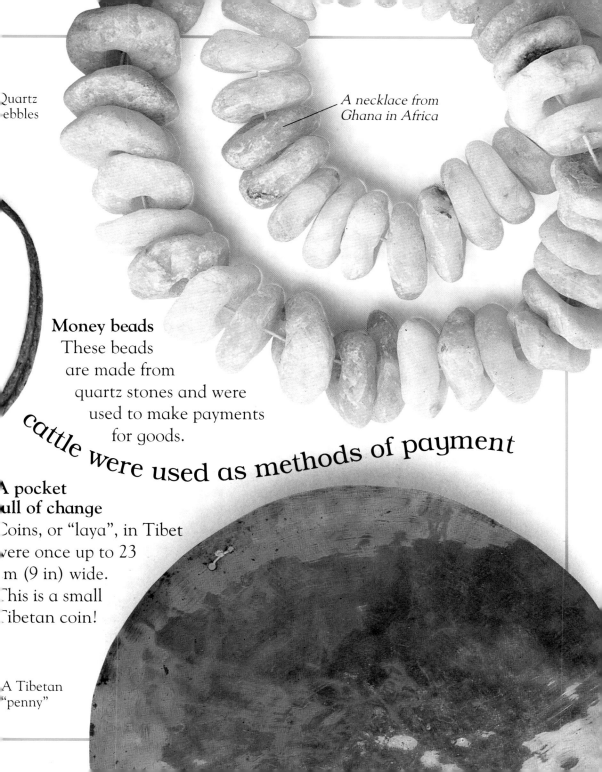

Quartz
pebbles

*A necklace from
Ghana in Africa*

Money beads
These beads
are made from
quartz stones and were
used to make payments
for goods.

cattle were used as methods of payment

**A pocket
full of change**
Coins, or "laya", in Tibet
were once up to 23
cm (9 in) wide.
This is a small
Tibetan coin!

A Tibetan
"penny"

Precious stones

The stones you kick around on a walk aren't valuable. But some stones, such as turquoise, agate, lapis, and jade, are rare and beautiful. They are used to make jewellery and precious ornaments.

Lapis comes from a Persian word meaning blue

Digging lapis

The best lapis of all comes from Afghanistan, where it is mined from quarries of white marble.

Lapis is easy to polish into beads for making necklaces

The name lapis comes from the Persian word "lazhward" which means "blue"

A gem called lapis

Lapis lazuli was used to decorate masks thousands of years ago in Babylon and Egypt. Its brilliant blue colour comes from small amounts of sulphur in the stone.

Jade

Jade is a hard stone that is very difficult to carve. But the Indians of Central America made many beautifully shaped jade objects.

Jade can be green, white, orange, brown, or lilac. It is most prized when it is emerald-green

Precious boulders

Jade occurs as jadeite and nephrite. It is often found in boulders that have been eroded by water.

Nephrite is usually green, grey, or creamy white

The Spanish call jade "hijada"

Trapped in time

Nature hides its own treasures. Animals die and become fossilized in rock. Insects may fall to a sticky end, to be trapped in amber for ever.

A glass coffin
Millions of years ago insects got stuck in oozing gum. Today they are perfectly preserved inside chunks that hardened into amber.

An insect preserved in amber

You can find fossils ...

Rocky resin
Amber looks and feels like a rock, but it is really the fossilized gum of coniferous trees.

Its glassy, yellow-brown colour makes amber good for jewellery

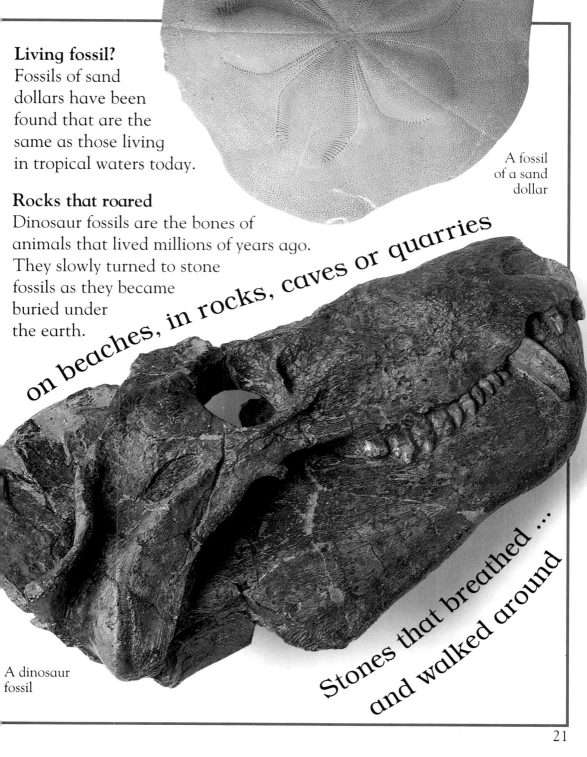

Living fossil?
Fossils of sand dollars have been found that are the same as those living in tropical waters today.

A fossil of a sand dollar

Rocks that roared
Dinosaur fossils are the bones of animals that lived millions of years ago. They slowly turned to stone fossils as they became buried under the earth.

on beaches, in rocks, caves or quarries

Stones that breathed ... and walked around

A dinosaur fossil

Treasure from the sea

Coral, shells, and pearls are made by sea animals. Pearl divers in Japan, known as *amas*, dive to depths of 12 m (40 ft) without breathing gear to collect pearl oysters.

The largest pearl in the ...

Pearly colours
Pearls can be gold, pink, or black in colour.

Annoyed oysters
Pearls are made when a grain of sand enters the shell of an oyster or mussel, irritating the animal. The grain is slowly coated with smooth layers of a substance called nacre to form the pearl.

Huge pearl oysters are found in the seas around Australia and Malaysia

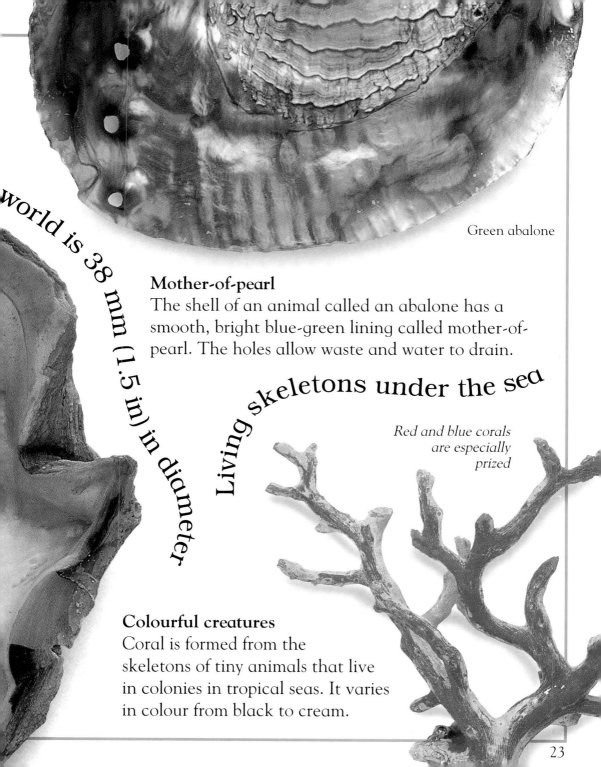

Green abalone

Mother-of-pearl
The shell of an animal called an abalone has a smooth, bright blue-green lining called mother-of-pearl. The holes allow waste and water to drain.

Living skeletons under the sea

*Red and blue corals
are especially
prized*

world is 38 mm (1.5 in) in diameter

Colourful creatures
Coral is formed from the skeletons of tiny animals that live in colonies in tropical seas. It varies in colour from black to cream.

Precious metals

Since the days of the ancient Egyptians, more than 5,000 years ago, gold and silver have been widely treasured. Today a third metal is even more valuable – platinum.

Fool's gold

Platinum

Platinum power
This metal has become very valuable because it is used by oil refineries, and also to reduce pollution from car exhausts.

Any fool's gold
"Fool's gold" is really iron pyrit Its bright, brass colour is easy to mistake for gold

There are over 80 ...

Solid gold tiara

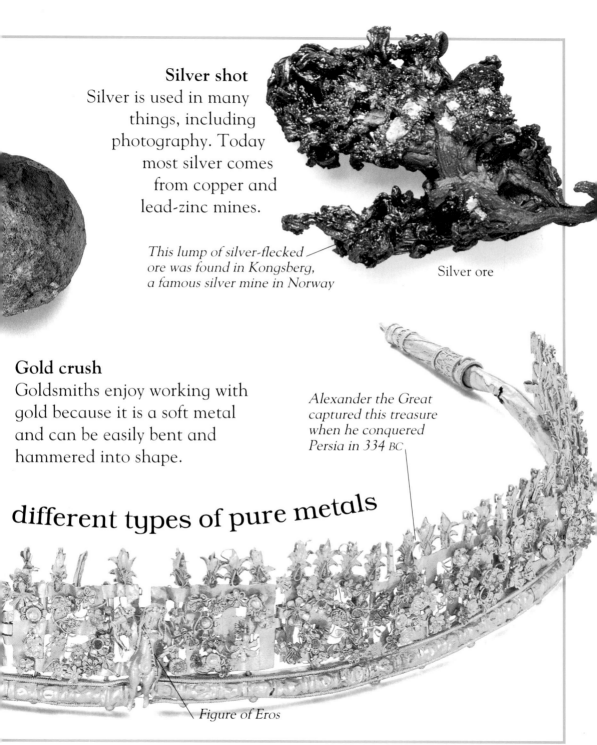

Silver shot
Silver is used in many things, including photography. Today most silver comes from copper and lead-zinc mines.

This lump of silver-flecked ore was found in Kongsberg, a famous silver mine in Norway

Silver ore

Gold crush
Goldsmiths enjoy working with gold because it is a soft metal and can be easily bent and hammered into shape.

Alexander the Great captured this treasure when he conquered Persia in 334 BC

different types of pure metals

Figure of Eros

Diamonds and gems

Diamond is the hardest of all known minerals, and the most valued, too. Its name comes from the Greek word *adamas,* which means unconquerable.

Deep diamonds

Diamonds are formed deep within the Earth's crust, under enormous pressure. Most of the world's best diamonds are mined in South Africa.

This gold snuffbox, made for Tsar Alexander II of Russia, is studded with 16 big diamonds

The actual size of the biggest diamond ever

King of the stones

This is a replica of the Cullinan diamond. It is the biggest diamond ever found. It weighs 3,016 carats and was discovered in a South African mine.

Ruby love

For a long time in Europe, red rubies were symbols of power and romance. They were often given as tokens of love.

Ruby

Amethyst

Gems are cut into special shapes

Amethyst ...hic!

In the past, some people believed that the purple stone amethyst cured drunkeness.

Amethyst

Some Egyptian emerald mines date back to 1500 BC

Emerald

Emeralds ...hiss!

Emeralds are a rich green colour and come mainly from South America. They were once thought to blind snakes.

Precious gems

Garnet

There are more than 3,000 kinds of minerals in nature, but only a few are rare, beautiful and hard enough to be cut into gems.

Tourmaline

Tourmaline comes in the widest range of colours of all gems. Its crystal shape leads to different colours even within the same stone. "Watermelon" tourmaline, for example, has a pink core and green outer edges.

All the colours of the rainbow

Zircon

Tourmaline

Zircon

Pure zircon is colourless and looks a lot like diamond. If zircon has a colour, it means the gem has impurities.

Spinel

Topaz

Spinel
Pure spinel is
clear, but metal traces
urn it pink, red, or green-blue.

Topaz
Topaz, especially golden topaz,
is largely found in Brazil. The
gem may also contain hints of
pink and blue.

*podumene crystals
are found in
California, Brazil,
and Afghanistan*

Chrysoberyl
brooch

Spodumene

Chrysoberyl

Chrysoberyl
This gem is the
third hardest in
the world after
diamond and corundum.
It is found in Brazil
and Sri Lanka in
yellow-green and
brown colours.

Almost as hard as diamond

Index

Five fiendish questions

1. Who was buried in a coffin of solid gold?

2. Which people first used gold and silver coins?

3. Where in the world could you once pay for things with dogs' teeth:
a) in Australia?
b) in Canada?
c) in China?
d) in Papua New Guinea?
e) in Hawaii?

4) What rare and beautiful treasure is yours if you find a boulder of nephrite?

5) What metal is more valuable than gold?

Answers on page 32

31

Answers

From page 30: 1. Tutankhamun, an ancient Egyptian pharaoh

2. The ancient Greeks

3. In Papua New Guinea, necklaces of dogs' teeth were used as money

4. Nephrite is the mineral from which we get jade

5. Platinum